Preface

Communication skills are essential for success in both academic and professional settings. They involve a range of competencies such as expressing ideas clearly, active listening, public speaking, group discussions, and the effective use of verbal and non-verbal communication. Understanding the significance of these skills in today's world, the Indira Gandhi National Open University (IGNOU) has included Communication Skills as a crucial part of the BCA curriculum, helping students enhance their overall personality and professional readiness.

"IGNOU BCA Communication Skills Previous Year Unsolved Papers MCS 015" is a thoughtfully curated collection of unsolved question papers from previous IGNOU examinations. This book is designed to help students become familiar with exam patterns, assess their preparation level, and develop a deeper understanding of communication concepts. Covering key areas like interpersonal communication, conflict resolution, and presentation skills, the book encourages active learning and critical thinking. We hope this compilation proves to be a valuable resource for exam preparation and a practical guide to mastering effective communication.

Index

Table of Contents

MCS-015: MCA (Revised)

Chapter 1: Term-End Examination, June- 2010

COMMUNICATION SKILLS (June 2010)

Time: 2 hours
Maximum Marks: 50
Note: Attempt all questions.

1. Read the following passage and answer the questions given below:

Mind you, I have often found that those using such arguments forget that science itself does not make discoveries purely by means of scientists exercising their powers of reasoning. Science makes progress through uncertain steps; it doesn't proceed from certainty to certainty but out of hypothesis that spring from intuition and which are then explored through experiments (And even when those experiments appear to confirm the original hypotheses, this by no means necessarily means that definite conclusions can be drawn from them.) Einstein once wrote: "The fairest thing we can experience is the mysterious. It is the fundamental emotion which stands at the cradle of true art and true science." Of course, Einstein was not denying the importance of reason, and nor would I suggest that reason was unimportant to him, but it would appear that for him there was more to the workings of science than pure reason. Although I hesitate to interpret Einstein's thought, to my mind he seems to be acknowledging that we can all experience the mysterious, that which is beyond reason.
(Mark Tully, India's Unending Journey)

(a) What is the point that the author is making in this paragraph? Tick the correct answer. 1
  Science is a mysterious phenomenon
  Science does not depend upon pure reason alone.
(b) What arguments would have been put forth by people, to which the author's responding in this paragraph? 2
(c) How does science make progress? 1
(d) Can everything be worked out and the outcome predicted? Why/why not? 2
(e) How can we say that science does not depend only upon pure reason? 2
(f) Use the word 'reason' as a noun and as a verb in sentences of your own. 2

2. Do as directed. **5**
(a) The grass is all wet. It (must have/could have) rained while we were sleeping.
(Select the correct modal)
(b) You (warn) not to repeat such a mistake in future. Any future occurrence will cost you dearly.
(Use the correct form of the verb)
(c) Radha told me about her job (that/which) she is enjoying very much.
(Select the correct word)
(d) Everyone (congratulate) Ali getting the first position.
(Use the correct form of the verb + correct preposition)

(e) The roads were damaged in the rains in 2007. They have not been repaired then. (Use a suitable word)

3. Develop a telephonic conversation Based on the information provided below, create a telephonic conversation between Mrs. Rana and an executive at the Sales Division of 'Tallwell Telephones.' Remember to begin with greetings. 10

Information Required by Mrs. Rana	**Information Provided by the Executive**
(a) New models available	(i) Two new models TW 1104 and TW 1120 with handsets
(b) Price of the telephone with handset	(ii) TW 1104 for Rs. 2000/- and TW 1120 with more features for Rs. 2800/-
(c) Teleconferencing facility	(iii) Available
(d) Memory	(iv) Can store up to 50 numbers

4. Write an application letter and prepare your CV.
(10 for the letter, 5 for the CV)

You are Akhilesh Chauhan. Write an application to Mr. Pravin Lobo, XYZ Publishing Co., Post Box: 4120, New Delhi, for the post of Senior Sales Executive in Rajasthan. Your details are as follows:

Prepare your CV in the correct format.

- Residential Address: 24, Tilak Nagar, Jaipur, Rajasthan
- Qualifications: B.Com, Diploma in Sales and Marketing
- Languages Proficient in: Hindi, English, Marathi, and Sindhi
- Experience: 2 years in selling academic books for a reputed publishing firm
- Interests: Traveling, meeting people
- Others: Hardworking

5. Write the text of a discussion. 10

The Heads of four divisions of an electronics company, namely Personnel, Production and Assembly, Sales and Marketing, and Maintenance, meet for a discussion on the after-effects of the global slowdown. Sales have dropped, and the funds have been reduced to 60% of what was received in the previous year. They discuss the possibilities of managing the situation and outcomes of the global slowdown. Write the text of the discussions.

MCA (Revised)

Chapter 2: Term-End Examination, June- 2011

MCS-015: COMMUNICATION SKILLS

Time: 2 hours
Maximum Marks: 50
Note: Answer all questions.

1. Read the following passage and answer the questions given after it. 10

Life is an examination in itself and education is the manifestation of the best in human beings. This is the key factor for an all-round personality development. Given this spirit, the effect of examinations in the educational system cannot be over-emphasized. Examinations determine not only what students learn, but also how they learn. It is important to recognize that the system of evaluation serves to establish a baseline by which improvement is measured. The examination content helps students acquire not only factual knowledge but also the attributes of a true education; eagerness to learn, adaptability to change, and the ability to think critically and communicate clearly.

Each year we are inundated by millions of students who must cope with ever-increasing amounts of theoretical knowledge as new topics and details emerge. The challenge is to improve the existing system so that it assesses more accurately the advanced skills students need in an increasingly competitive world. Many of our national leaders, past and present, have been passionately committed to education. They have pioneered mass education, literacy movements, and extensive higher learning. But other countries are able to achieve higher academic levels. Why can't we? The reason is simple: pressures and obstacles upset people. There is a nervous hurry when the examination dates draw near. Predicted examination content is studied to the exclusion of other learning. We make examinations the end of education and not an accessory in its acquisition.

Questions:
(a) What does education reveal in human beings? 1
(b) What do examinations determine? 1
(c) Enumerate the features of true education. 2
(d) There are different challenges facing the examination system. Discuss. 2
(e) What has been the commitment of our national leaders to education? 2
(f) Give antonyms (opposites) of the following words used in the passage: 2

- Simple
- Exclusion

2. Fill in the blanks choosing the most suitable phrasal verb from those given below: 5

Make changes in the form of the verb where necessary. There is one extra phrasal verb.
Phrasal verbs: get out, turn up, deal with, pick up, put off, give up.
(a) The meeting ____ the problem of the striking workers.
(b) Can you ____ me up at the station?

(c) He is trying to ____ smoking. He is determined to do that.
(d) I love this song. Do you mind if I ____ the volume?
(e) I am afraid the situation is ____ hand.

3. Write down the text of a group discussion between four participants on the issue of domestic violence and ways to control this. 10

4. Write a letter of application along with your Curriculum Vitae (C.V) for the job of a Tele-Caller Executive in response to the following advertisement: 15

Advertisement:
Position: Tele-Caller Executive
Job profile: Knowledge of Kotak products and procedures. Handling inbound and outbound calls to answer overseas customer queries.
Skills: Graduation degree, Excellent Communication skills in English, negotiating skills.
Apply within 7 days to Modern Consultants Ltd, Nehru Place, New Delhi 110017.

5. You are Aakash Mehra, Sales Manager, Kotak Mahindra Bank, New Delhi. Write a memo to be sent to all the Sales Executives to attend a meeting on 2nd July and to give a detailed account of the targets achieved by them in the last quarter. 10

MCA (Revised)

Chapter 3: Term-End Examination, June- 2012

MCS-015: COMMUNICATION SKILLS

Time: 2 hours
Maximum Marks: 50
Note: Answer all questions.

1. Read the following passage and answer the questions given after it. **10**

Parkour is a new sport that has caught the fancy of quite a few people, young and old alike. Parkour means free running. It is a physical discipline of French origin. Those who participate in it are called traceurs. They combine 'sport' and 'art' to perform daring feats. The underlying principle is to get from Point A to Point B in the minimum possible time using whatever one has got. Jumping from rooftop to rooftop and sliding down railings are all a form of Parkour.

It is an extreme sport with a high risk of injuries. But the best thing is that it can be practised just about anywhere.Anyone can do Parkour. But for those who are interested in martial arts, Parkour is a must since it builds up stamina and strengthens the body. It boosts self-confidence too.Those who practise Parkour largely depend upon the Internet or videos of Parkour for their training. This is because the sport is not yet very popular in India and hence trainers are not too many.

Questions:

(a) What does Parkour mainly comprise? 1
(b) In what ways is Parkour an 'extreme' sport? 2
(c) Does Parkour require any equipment? Why or why not? 2
(d) Which kind of people benefit most from Parkour? Why? 2
(e) Parkour incorporates both sport and ______ (complete the sentence). 1
(f) Where are instructors of Parkour to be found? Why? 2

2. Do as directed. **5**

(a) You'd like to know why the tenders have not been opened.
(Make a 'wh' question)
(b) Maria has to ______________ (handle/cope) with all kinds of difficult situations in the office.
(Select the appropriate word)
(c) Speak only if you have something sensible to say______________keep quiet and listen to what others are saying.
(Use a suitable connector)
(d) You mustn't/may not/needn't come to the office tomorrow if you are unwell. I can manage.
(Select the appropriate modal)

(e) We enclose a copy of rules and regulations with this letter.
(Rewrite in the passive voice)

3. Write a letter of acceptance to the appointment letter carrying the details given below. **10**

- **Company:** Silverline Tours and Travels, 30-B, Upsara Towers, Bara Khamba Road, New Delhi - 110001.
- **Dated:** 22 December 2011
- **Post:** Executive, Marketing Division•
- **Starting Salary:** Rs. 20,000/- per month
- **Joining Date:** 1 January 2012
- **Signed by:** GM, Silverline Tours and Travels

4. Write a letter of application along with your Curriculum Vitae (CV) for the job of Animator and Illustrator in response to the advertisement given below. 10

Position: Animator and Illustrator
Skills and qualifications required:

- Graduate in Multimedia Animation from a UGC-recognized institute
- Knowledge of Adobe, Photoshop, Illustrator, Corel Draw, Flash, Web Weaver, etc.

Experience: At least 3 years in a multimedia and animation company.
Job Profile: Animation and illustration, Web designing.

5. Prepare a report on the modernization of your seminar room based on the notes provided below. 15

Your Department Head has asked you to prepare a report. Expand the notes into a full report.
Notes:

- Seepage to be checked
- Repainting of the walls
- Old windows to be replaced
- New furniture
- Split air-conditioner to be installed
- Whiteboard and projection system

MCA (Revised)

Chapter 4: Term-End Examination, December- 2012

MCS-015: COMMUNICATION SKILLS

Time: 2 hours
Maximum Marks: 50
Note: Answer all questions.

1. Read the following passage and answer the questions given after it. **10**

The impressive capability for understanding of parrots and corvines (crows, jays, ravens, and jackdaws) has been extensively documented in scientific literature. These two have a large brain relative to body size. Apparently, this is true of all mammals that exhibit greater cognitive development.

In the case of crows, which generally rank very low in human esteem, the relative size of the brain is the same as that of chimpanzees. But the size of the brain alone does not translate to higher cognitive capability, i.e., the ability to think and understand. It is the presence of a larger forebrain where memory, thought, and action are located, that makes these birds intelligent.

Scientists have attempted to compare the levels of cognition and problem-solving skills of parrots and crows. They used a combination of four tests, two of which involved tool-use. Overall, the kea parrots performed much better than the crows. While none of the crows employed more than one solution, the kea parrots were quicker in discovering multiple solutions.

Questions:
(a) Say whether the statements given below are true or false. 4
(i) Parrots and crows can be classified as corvids.
(ii) If an animal has a large brain size, it is expected to be more intelligent.
(iii) The brain of a crow is as large as that of a chimpanzee.
(iv) An animal or bird's use of a tool indicates the ability to think and understand.

(b) What brain functions are located in the forebrain? 2
(c) What kind of tests were used to judge and compare the cognitive level of crows and parrots? 2
(d) In what way did the kea parrots prove to be superior to the crows? 2

2. Do as directed. **5**

(a) There is still much to discuss. We shall ______ return to this item at our next meeting. *(Use a suitable connector)*
(b) They have not responded to our offer. They can't/mustn't/shouldn't be interested. *(Select the appropriate modal)*

(c) Using better-trained staff can increase productivity. *(Begin with 'Productivity can'----------)*
(d) I would like to attract the attention of the Board to/at point no.15 of the charter. *(Select the appropriate preposition)*
(e) The efficiency of the staff is due to ______ immense work pressure. *(Improving/ declining)*
(Select the appropriate word)

3. Write down the text of a group discussion involving four participants on increasing security measures in their office. 15

You may include some of the ideas given below:

- Security check at all entrances
- Reducing the number of entry points
- Restricting visitors to the lobby near reception
- Providing identified visitors with "visitor's pass"
- Maintaining a visitor's register

4. Write a letter of application along with your Curriculum Vitae (CV) for the job of a Product Manager in a Publishing House. 10

Advertisement:
Position: Product Manager, Science & Maths School Books
Qualification:

- Degree in Science or Mathematics
- MBA in Marketing

Technical Experience:

- Experience of teaching maths or science

Job Profile:

- Making review proposals
- Providing feedback during product development
- Effective marketing
- Making new market plans

5. Write a memo as Ravi Parasher, Executive, HR Department, Surya Chemicals, Chennai, to Ms. Rezia Begum, Senior Manager, R&D Division, about the arrangement for the visit of Dr. T.R. Rao from Mumbai on January 20, 2012. 10

MCA (Revised)

Chapter 5: Term-End Examination, June- 2013

MCS-015: COMMUNICATION SKILLS

Time: 2 hours
Maximum Marks: 50
Note: Answer all questions.

1. Read the following passage and answer the questions given below it. 10

Koduvally village near Kozhikode in north Kerala has nearly forgotten its tradition of pottery-making. Today, it is known as the state's "gold village," boasting more than 100 jewellery shops. Their clientele: hundreds of families who have relatives working in the Gulf.

In spite of skyrocketing prices of the yellow metal - from Rs 4,395 per 10 gram in 2000 to more than Rs 20,000 in 2011 - its demand has not been seriously affected in Kerala. The south Indian states alone account for 60 percent of gold sales in India, the world's biggest gold consumer.

According to industry sources, Kerala tops the country in gold consumption, with the largest number of retailers - more than 5,000 compared to 1,000 a decade ago. The state consumes about 75 tonnes - valued at about Rs 20,000 crore - of the 650 tonnes of gold sold in India every year and is home to some of Asia's largest gold showrooms. And it's not just the urban parts of the state where swanky, mammoth showrooms are coming up every day; even the villages are witnessing the gold rush with showrooms covering up to 35,000 sq ft.

This huge demand is attributed to the growing remittances - Rs 40,000 crore annually - by its 20 lakh-strong non-residents based in the Gulf and the US. Another reason is the steep increase in prices of rubber in the last 10 years, from Rs 25 per kg to Rs 225 per kg, which is bringing a windfall to Kerala farmers who produce 92 percent of India's natural rubber.

Questions:

(a) Say whether the following statements are True (T) or False (F). *4*

(i) Once upon a time, pottery making was the main occupation of the people of Koduvally.
(ii) The people of Koduvally buy gold mainly from Gulf countries.
(iii) Kerala is the biggest consumer of gold in the world.
(iv) The number of retail gold sellers has gone up from 1000 to 5000 in 10 years.

(b) Answer the following questions: *2*

(i) Mention the two biggest sources of money in Kerala which enable them to buy gold.
(ii) Which part of India is the biggest consumer of gold?

(c) Find words from the passage which are close in meaning to the following words/phrases: 2

- Flashy

- Very large
- Money sent to someone at a distance
- An unexpected piece of good fortune

(d) Find words from the passage which are opposite in meaning to the following words: 2

- Rural
- Gentle

2. Do as directed: ***5***

(a) The missing file (was, had been) found in the drawer.
(Choose the correct word/phrase)

(b) The stationery available in the local market is the ________.
(Use the correct form of "cheap")

(c) Form a question to which the following may be the answer:
"The Chief Minister was interviewed by Barkha Dutt."

(d) Mr. Khanna was asked to explain why he was late.
(Rewrite in the active voice)

(e) Dogs are faithful animals, ________.
(Supply a question tag)

3. Letter Writing: **10**

As the Purchase Manager of a garment factory, you purchased 1000 balls of silk material from Tushar Silk Mills, Surat. On delivery, it was found that at least 30% of the material had weaving or printing defects. Write a letter to the supplier stating the details of defects and asking them to provide a replacement and compensation for the inconvenience and loss of time.

4. Job Application and CV Writing: **15**

You are an M.Com and MBA graduate from Nagpur University. Apply to HDFC Bank for the post of an Assistant Manager. Mention a few other qualities of yours that would be helpful for this job. Enclose a Curriculum Vitae (CV) along with the application.

5. Construct a Telephonic Conversation: **10**

You are a Receptionist at Hotel Rain Tree in Chennai. Construct a telephonic conversation with a client who wants to seek information regarding the kind of accommodation available, the tariff, corporate discount, pick-up facilities, etc. You must write 10 turns of the conversation.

MCA (Revised)

Chapter 6: Term-End Examination, December- 2013

MCS-015: COMMUNICATION SKILLS

Time: 2 hours
Maximum Marks: 30
Note: Answer all questions.

1. Read the following passage given below and answer the questions after it. **10**

Many aspects of the modern age began in Britain - railways, industry, seaside resorts, weekend holidays, and organised sports. Of the latter, perhaps the most successful has been the game of association football, or soccer as it is now more widely known.Different ideas have been put forward as to the earliest origins of the game. It seems likely that it began as a ritual battle between rival villages, the object of which was to win and keep possession of an inflated pig's bladder. The game has since evolved into one of great elegance and skill and is not, as some might think, simply a matter of twenty-two men trying to kick a ball into a net.

Until the 1950s, when the players were mainly working men from the local community who held ordinary jobs by day and trained in the evenings for the Saturday match, the maximum wage per game was fixed at a modest twenty pounds. However, those days are long gone, and nowadays soccer is a major international business. Outstanding players enjoy the status of celebrities and are transferred from club to club for multi-million pound fees.Every Saturday, worldwide, millions of devoted supporters crowd through the gates of their local stadium to watch their heroes in action. Of course, there is nothing new in this, for in ancient Greece and Rome thousands filled the amphitheatres to watch games and contests. But why, one may ask, do so many football enthusiasts choose to risk the discomfort of crowds and bad weather when they could watch the big match live on television in the comfort of their own homes? The answer, we are told, is that there is no substitute for the atmosphere of the stadium, where the roar of the crowd is medicine against the stresses of the working week for football fans around the globe.

Questions:

(a) Where do you think the sport in question originated? What do you know about its beginnings? 2

(b) Choose the correct option: 1

The writer thinks that the sport in its initial stages was:

(i) rather crude

(ii) elegant

(iii) a means of evoking emotions

(c) Say whether the following statements are True (T) or False (F). 3

(i) The game's popularity is restricted to Britain.

(ii) Soccer players have always been rich and famous.

(iii) In the writer's opinion, it is better to watch the match on TV than go to the stadium.

(d) Find words in the passage which mean the same as those given below: 2

(i) Replacement

(ii) Developed
(iii) Competing
(iv) Loyal

(e) Find words in the passage which mean the opposite of the following: 2
(i) End
(ii) Ordinary/common
(iii) Ancient
(iv) Local

2. Do as directed: 5

(a) Fill in the blanks with the suitable form of the verb given in brackets: "Yesterday 15 flights (had been coming, came) late because of the heavy rain."

(b) Write a question to which the following may be an answer:
"Only 6 members attended the meeting."

(c) The secretary wrote the minutes of the meeting.
(Rewrite in the passive voice)

(d) It is more easier to use the word processor than the typewriter.
(Rewrite it correctly)

(e) The prices of vegetables have gone up, ________.
(Write a question tag)

3. Letter Writing: **10**

As the librarian of a school, you placed an order for 5 copies of Longman's Dictionary of Contemporary English with Messers Girdhari Lal and Son. On delivery, you found that in one of the copies, 43 pages are missing, one copy is an old edition, the price of which is 20% less than the latest edition (as required by you). Write a letter of complaint to the concerned dealer asking him to make amends for the gross mistake.

4. Job Application and CV Writing: **10**

You are Nishant Bajaj, an M.Com graduate pursuing Chartered Accountancy. Write an application to Punjab Tractors for the post of Finance Manager. Enclose a Curriculum Vitae (CV) along with the application.

5. Construct a Telephonic Conversation: **10**

You are a receptionist in a bank. Construct a telephonic conversation with a client who wants to seek information regarding the facilities for a car loan, the terms and conditions, the time frame for repayment, the rate of interest, and the optimum time required for the process. You must take 10 turns of the conversation.

MCA (Revised)/BCA (Revised)

Chapter 7: Term-End Examination, June- 2014

MCS-015: COMMUNICATION SKILLS

Time: 2 hours
Maximum Marks: 50
Note: Answer all questions.

1. Read the following passage and answer the questions given after it. **10**

Nehru felt that as he matured and experienced life, he had grown less confident of the path towards his long cherished ideals. In the later phase of his life, he was making a more realistic assessment of human weaknesses and the problems in the way of progress.Yet he retained his faith in the force or spirit of man, that had somehow guided human beings. In a changing world, Nehru was convinced that humankind was in crucial need of an active and positive philosophy or way of thinking. Neither religious systems nor spiritualism with their unexplained assumptions were acceptable to him. Nor were philosophical speculations with their focus on the abstract. Even Marxism and Leninism were found to be wanting because of their doctrinal rigidity and lack of ethical means.

Nehru did not claim that there was a single philosophy or doctrine for human development. He stated that he appreciated an ethical approach to human life which was also scientific and objective so as to build a human culture that satisfied both spiritual and physical needs. In a fast changing world where there were few certainties, these were to be valuable guidelines.

Questions:

(a) What does the narrator feel about Nehru's point of view on life in his later years 2
(b) What issues/difficulties did Nehru find with Marxism and Leninism? 2
(c) Which philosophy of life did Nehru appear to be fond of? 2
(d) Pick out synonyms of the following words from the passage: 2
(i) Evaluation
(ii) Vital
(e) Pick out antonyms of the following words from the passage: 2
(i) Earlier
(ii) Concrete

2. Do as directed: **5**

(a) The Board of Management meeting has been postponed due to the volatile market condition.
(Make a 'wh' question)

(b) Radha has to (look after/look for) her parents in her free time. *(Select the appropriate word)*

(c) The school is celebrating its Annual Day next week. *(Rewrite in the passive voice)*

(d) All of us need to/must/should/ought to respect the traffic lights even at night. *(Select the appropriate modal)*

(e) The rate of inflation is very high. The common man has to face a lot of difficulty to make both ends meet. *(Combine these sentences)*

3. Write a letter of acceptance for the post and company given below: **10**
Company: New Media Pvt. Ltd.
Address: 191, New Videocon Towers, Bara Khamba Road, New Delhi - 110001
Dated: 10 June 2011
Post: Marketing Executive
Starting Salary: Rs 25,000/- per month
Joining Date: 17 June 2011
Signed by: MD, New Media Pvt Ltd.

4. Write an application giving your Curriculum Vitae (CV) for the post of Creative Designer in response to the advertisement given below: 10

Position: Creative Designer
Qualification: Graduation or more in animation design with professional knowledge of Adobe Photoshop, Corel Draw, and Web Weaver
Experience: Minimum 3 years in a reputed company
Job Profile: Creating designs for leading MNCs
Salary: As per the market norms

5. Prepare a report on the Annual Prize Distribution function which was held in your College/Institution. 10

MCA (Revised)/BCA (Revised)

Chapter 8: Term-End Examination, December- 2014

MCS-015: COMMUNICATION SKILLS

Time: 2 hours
Maximum Marks: 50
Note: Answer all questions.

1. Read the following passage and answer the questions given after it. **10**

The lives of people all over the world are generally influenced by the climate of the country in which they live. For example, climatic conditions have an effect on the sort of clothes people wear. In a cold climate, warm clothes are required, and materials for making such clothes are provided by the animals found in cold countries. Similarly, people in hot countries wear silk and cotton, which grows easily in hot climates. Climate also decides the type of houses people live in; in hot climates, flat roofs and wide verandahs are suitable, but in cold countries, sloping roofs and thick walls are required. Food is also the product of climatic conditions. People eat what is easily cultivated.

In general, the hottest parts of the world are those nearest to the Equator, but other factors also have an influence upon climate. Distance from the sea is important since it will influence temperature, rainfall, and humidity. Height is also a vital factor. Places at high altitude are always cooler than places at sea level in the same latitude. Physical features such as mountains, which may stop the passage of cold winds and cause rainfall, also have an effect on the climate.

Questions:
(a) In what ways does the climate influence the lives of people in a country? 2
(b) Who provides the materials for warm clothes in a cold climate? 2
(c) How does the altitude of a place influence its climate? 2
(d) What type of houses are suitable for people in a hot climate? 2
(e) In what ways do physical features influence the climate of a place? 2

2. Do as directed: **5**
(i) The dog jumped ____ the table. *(on/upon)*
(ii) She was married ____ the age of twenty. *(in/at)*
(iii) The weather of Delhi is warm ____ than that of Amritsar. *(Correct the sentence)*
(iv) India lifted the Cricket World Cup in 2011. *(Change to passive voice)*
(v) Hind Swaraj was written in the year 1909. *(Add a question tag)*

3. Write a letter of acceptance with a request for relaxation for a month in the joining period. The details of the company and the job are given below: 10

Company: New Horizons Pvt. Ltd.
Address: 187, Paharganj, New Delhi
Dated: 15 June, 2011
Post: Head, Sales Division
Starting Salary: Rs 35,000/- per month
Joining Date: 22 June, 2011
Signed by: Director, New Horizons Pvt. Ltd.

4. What is the difference between note-taking and keeping minutes of a meeting? Write an extended note on the process of minute-taking and why it is necessary to keep minutes of a meeting. 10

5. Prepare a report on the Tech-expo which you visited recently. 10
Below are the notes that you may use for your report:

- 15 June, Pragati Maidan, New Delhi
- Inauguration by Prime Minister
- Attended by a host of national and international delegates
- Display of new technologies from many countries
- P-V, VI series attracted everybody

MCA (Revised)/BCA (Revised)

Chapter 9: Term-End Examination, June- 2015

MCS-015: COMMUNICATION SKILLS

Time: 2 hours
Maximum Marks: 50
Note: Answer all questions.

1. Read the following passage and answer the questions given after it. **10**

Growing at an annual compound rate of 40% for the past five years, the Information Technology industry has become one of the largest foreign exchange earners in India. During this period, growth achieved by the IT industry seems unattainable for many others in the current economic scenario.

The past five years have seen the Indian IT industry go through fundamental changes. Earlier, the IT industry was equated with hardware, which was then the major bread earner. But now software accounts for more than half of the industry's total revenue. The transition has not happened overnight. Some factors aiding the downfall of the hardware sector have been the following: Lack of government spending, adverse policies, and the Y2K problem which has pumped in millions of dollars into software. The hardware sector, faced with huge tariffs, was forced into a corner in the early nineties when manufacturing became unviable. This goaded Indian hardware companies into joint ventures with international majors for marketing their products in India. The sector still faces stiff competition from the unorganized sector.

Questions:
(i) Give a suitable title for the passage. 2
(ii) What is unique about the IT industry in the present economic scenario? 2
(iii) Why did the IT industry go through a fundamental change? 2
(iv) What are the major factors responsible for the downfall of the hardware sector? 2
(v) Pick out suitable synonyms from the passage for the following words: yearly, vital, change, compelled. 2

2. Fill in the blanks choosing the most suitable phrasal verb from those given below: 5
(Make changes in the form of the verbs where necessary)
Phrasal Verbs: blow up, ask around, bring up, chip in, get along, fall down.

(i) I ____ but nobody had seen my wallet.
(ii) The racing car ____ after it crashed into the fence.
(iii) His grandparents ____ him after the death of his parents.
(iv) If everyone ____, we can get the kitchen painted by noon.
(v) I was surprised how well my new girlfriend and my sister ____

3. Write down the text of a group discussion between three participants on the issue of 'Changing Role of Indian Women'. 10

4. Write a letter of application along with your Curriculum Vitae (CV) for the job of a Tele-caller in response to the following advertisement: 10

Position: Tele-caller
Job Profile: Graduation Degree
Good Communication Skills
Knowledge of Company's profile and products, i.e., HCL

5. You are Akshat Khanna, Head, Publicity Division, Hindustan Times. Write a memo to all the sales executives to come for a review meeting on July 20th with a detailed activity report of all the assignments and targets achieved by them in the last quarter. 10

MCA (Revised) / BCA (Revised)

Chapter 10: Term-End Examination, December- 2015

MCS-015: COMMUNICATION SKILLS

Time: 2 hours
Maximum Marks: 50
Note: Answer all questions.

1. Read the following passage and answer the questions given after it. **10**

The telecom services have been recognized the world-over as an important tool for socio-economic development for a nation. It is one of the prime support services needed for rapid growth and modernization of various sectors of the economy. The Indian telecommunication sector has undergone a major process of transformation through significant policy reforms, particularly beginning with the announcement of NTP 1994, which was subsequently re-emphasized and carried forward under NTP 1999. Driven by various policy initiatives, the Indian telecom sector witnessed a complete transformation in the last decade. It has achieved a phenomenal growth in recent years and is poised to take a big leap in the future as well.

The Indian Telecommunications Network, with 621 million connections (as on March 2011), is the third largest in the world. The sector has been growing at a speed of 45% in recent years. This rapid growth is possible due to various proactive and positive decisions of the Government and the contribution of both the public and the private sectors. The rapid strides in the telecom sector have been facilitated by the liberal policies that provide easy market access for telecom equipment and a fair regulatory framework for offering telecom services to the Indian consumers at affordable prices.

Questions:
(a) Suggest a suitable title for the passage. 2
(b) What is the role of telecommunications in the growth of an economy? 2
(c) What has led to the mass changes in the Indian telecommunications scenario? 2
(d) Pick out from the passage synonyms for the following words: significant, fast, section, change. 2
(e) Pick out from the passage antonyms (opposite) for the following words: minor, insignificant, smallest, conservative. 2

2. Fill in the blanks choosing the most suitable phrasal verb from those given below: 5
(Make changes in the form of the verbs where necessary)
Phrasal Verbs: look after, give up, turn down, show off, wear off, work out

(a) The Umpire ____ the enthusiastic appeal from the bowler.
(b) One should never ____ one's efforts in pursuit of excellence.
(c) He always ____ his wealth.
(d) Most of her make-up ____ before she reached the party.
(e) The grandmother ____ the child while the family was away.

3. Write down the text of a group discussion between three participants on the issue of 'Increasing Violence against Women'. 10

4. Write a letter of application along with your Curriculum Vitae (C.V.) for the job of a Marketing Executive in response to the following advertisement: 10

Position: Marketing Executive
Skills: Graduation degree, excellent communication skills in English, negotiation skills, willingness to travel
Job Profile: Knowledge of Tata Industries and procedures and complete information on Tata products and Indian market

5. You are Krishna Mehra, Finance Head of ANZ Bank, New Delhi. Write a memo to all the Sales Executives to come for a review meeting on 10th August with a detailed account of the targets achieved by them in the last quarter. 10

MCA (Revised) / BCA (Revised)

Chapter 11: Term-End Examination, June- 2016

MCS-015: COMMUNICATION SKILLS

Time: 2 hours
Maximum Marks: 50
Note: Answer all questions.

1. Read the passage given below and answer the questions that follow: 10

A client was working with a set goal to enroll three customers within 90 days for his new Internet business. Each week, he took the steps necessary to help him achieve his goal. And, each week he was one step closer to accomplishing his goal. The end of his target was drawing near, and he still had two customers to enroll. His deadline passed without achieving his goal. Even though he had many potential customers, there were some details he had to work out first, which he hadn't originally thought of. Therefore, in his mind, he decided he had failed in achieving his goal. He was very disappointed and became discouraged and de-motivated. And consequently, he completely missed the success that was buried in his perceived 'failure'.

I suggested he takes a look at the life of Bill Gates. Certainly, he had his share of 'failures' along the way. When he failed to reach one of his goals, did he let that stop him? Absolutely not! Gates re-evaluated the goal, re-grouped, and revised. And, you can bet he didn't do this all on his own. He asked his key people to help. Gates recognized that successful people look at what's worked, learn from what hasn't, set new priorities, and then move on. You don't see them dragging their 'failures' into work with them every morning. Gates is where he is because he knows the importance of looking for the success in the 'failure'.

My client then put on this 'Bill Gates hat'. He re-evaluated the goal he had set and realized that had it not been for the actions he had already taken, he wouldn't have known he had to shore up his business infrastructure in order to be ready for his new customers. What first looked like a failure was actually a success. Once he took the time to reflect on and recognize the success in his 'failure', he was able to re-group and revise his strategy to reach his goal. He was now back on his way to achieving success ... from the inside out.

(a) Why was the 'client' not able to achieve his goal? 2
(b) What do you understand by the phrase 'success buried in his failure'? 2
(c) What was the secret of Bill Gates' success? 2
(d) Explain the phrase 'put on his Bill Gates hat'. 2
(e) Find words in the passage which mean the same as: 2
  (i) as a result
  (ii) plan of action

2. Do as directed: 5

(a) The bell has been rung.
(Rewrite in the active voice)

(b) Three months ago he (be) sentenced to rigorous imprisonment.
(Put the correct form of the verb in the brackets)

(c) I have disposed off my car.
(Rewrite correctly)

(d) I am going to (take, give) my higher secondary exam next year.
(Choose the correct option in the brackets)

(e) You can't get good marks unless you don't work hard.
(Rewrite the sentence correctly)

3. Conversation Writing: **10**

A reputed firm is interested in placing an order for 100 computers. Write a conversation between the Marketing Manager of HCL and a sales representative of Tech India who wants to seek information regarding the availability of computers, maximum time for delivery, discount for bulk purchase, after-sales service, and time limit for payment. You must take ten turns.

4. Job Application Writing: **15**

You are Nidhi Khanna. You have completed an MBA course. Write an application for the post of Finance Executive of Brick World Pvt. Ltd. Enclose a C.V. along with the letter of application.

5. Essay Writing: **10**

Enumerate the qualities required to become a good negotiator in order to run one's business successfully.

MCA (Revised) / BCA (Revised)

Chapter 12: Term-End Examination, December- 2016

MCS-015: COMMUNICATION SKILLS

Time: 2 hours
Maximum Marks: 50
Note: Attempt all questions.

1. Read the following passage and answer the questions given below: 10

I have been particularly influenced by a sustained association with Mazdoor Kisan Shakti Sangathan (MKSS) in Rajasthan and, more recently, with Akal Sangharsh Samiti. The latter is an all Rajasthan network of about 50 grassroot organizations that came together in late 2000 to defend the rights of drought-affected people, especially the right to employment. This campaign involved a good deal of action-oriented (even 'action-based') research, focusing, for instance, on living conditions in drought-affected areas, the government's response to the crisis, and corruption in relief works.

My association with this campaign was an eye-opening experience in many ways. I discovered, for instance, that my painstakingly accumulated academic baggage was not always as useful as I had expected in this venture. After 15 years of research on hunger and famines, one is perhaps entitled to feel like an 'expert' of sorts on these matters. Yet I did not always find myself better equipped than others to understand the practical issues that arose in this situation. At times, I even felt embarrassingly ignorant compared with local people who had little formal education but sharp understanding of the real world. Some of them were curious about my collaborative work with Amartya Sen (who had become a household name in India after winning the Nobel Prize in Economics), but when I tried to explain to them the main insights of this work, they were not exactly impressed. Though they did not disagree, there was no enthusiasm in their approval, no acknowledgment of depth or importance.

(a) What made Mazdoor Kisan Shakti Sangathan and Akal Sangharsh Samiti come together? 2

(b) What was the focus of their campaign? 2

(c) What did the writer of the passage learn from the campaign? 2

(d) Give a suitable title to the passage. 2

(e) (i) Pick out, from the text, the opposite of the word 'former'. 1

(ii) What do you think is the meaning of the phrase 'an eye-opening experience'? 1

2. Do as directed: 5

(a) The tourist facilities (improve) considerably in the Eastern zone since last year. *(Write the verb in brackets in the correct tense)*

(b) I am having five dictionaries.
(Rewrite correctly)

(c) We have enclosed the payment along with the order.
(Rewrite in the passive voice)

(d) She is too old to cope with the stress of the modern lifestyle.
(Rewrite after removing 'too')

(e) She said, "I want to go to Chandigarh tomorrow."
(Rewrite in indirect speech)

3. Letter Writing: **10**

As a client, you have not been able to repay the loan taken from your bank in the stipulated time, and the bank has charged a penal interest. Write a letter to the Bank Manager requesting him to waive off the additional interest/penalty.

4. Minutes Writing: **15**

As the Company Secretary of Engineers India Limited, write the minutes of a recently held meeting of the sales team.

5. Conversation Writing: **10**

You are a librarian in a public library. Write a conversation with a visitor who wants to seek information regarding the terms and conditions of membership, the amount of security deposit, annual subscription, number of books issued at a time, and the period of issue. You must take 10 turns.

MCA (Revised) / BCA (Revised)

Chapter 13: Term-End Examination, June- 2017

MCS-015: COMMUNICATION SKILLS

Time: 2 hours
Maximum Marks: 50
Note: Answer all questions.

1. Read the following passage and answer the questions given below: **10**

Life is an examination in itself, and education is the manifestation of the best in human beings: the key factor for an all-round personality development. Given this spirit, the effect of examinations cannot be overemphasized. Examinations determine not only what students learn but also how they learn. It is important to recognize that this system of evaluation serves to establish a baseline by which improvement is measured. The examination content helps students acquire not only factually important knowledge but also the attributes of true education: eagerness to learn, adaptability to change, and the ability to think critically and communicate clearly.

Each year we are inundated by millions of students who must cope with ever-increasing amounts of theoretical knowledge as new topics and details emerge. The challenge is to improve the existing system so that it assesses more accurately the advanced skills students need in an increasingly competitive world. Many of our national leaders, past and present, have been passionately committed to the cause of education. They have pioneered mass education and literacy movements and extensive higher learning. But other countries are able to achieve higher academic levels and goals, so why can't we? The reason is simple: pressure and obstacles upset people. There is a nervous hurry when the examination dates draw near. Predicted examination content is studied, which leads to a diminished learning pattern. We make the examination the end of education and not an accessory in its acquisition.

(a) What does education reveal in human beings? 2
(b) What do examinations determine? 2
(c) How is improvement measured through examinations? 2
(d) What are the features of 'true education'? 2
(e) What are the challenges facing the examination system? 2
(f) Give antonyms of the following words used in the passage: 2
Life, higher, simple,near

2. Do as directed: **5**

(a) They are repairing the roads.
(Rewrite in the passive voice)

(b) Mr. Anand owns a house in the NCR region. He built it in 1989.
(Combine the two sentences)

(c) A good teacher (should not/might not) ignore any pupil in his/her class.
(Choose the correct option)

(d) Shakespeare is one of the best poets of English literature.
(Correct the sentence)

(e) Many Indian citizens find it difficult to make ends meet.
(Choose the correct word: both/all)

3. Rewrite the following sentences, removing the error, if any: 5
(a) When not used, all spare equipments should be put away.
(b) You can expect a flood in November in Southern India.
(c) There is a mail for you at the office.
(d) Avantika sits besides me in class while Sita sits behind me.
(e) She has just went to the meeting at the Municipal hall.

4. CV and Cover Letter Writing: 10
Prepare your Curriculum Vitae (CV) along with a covering (forwarding) letter in response to the advertisement given below:

Position: Team Leader (Software Department, Tata Infotech)
Qualification: Bachelor in Business Administration/BCA with Industry knowledge
Experience: 3 years (minimum) in a registered company
Job Profile: Leading a team of 10–15 people in the concerned department
Salary: As per market standards

5. Report Writing: 10
Prepare a report of the Industrial trade fair that you recently visited with a particular focus on the software companies and their participation. Write down the benefits that accrue from such visits.

6. Minutes Writing: 10
Write a brief note on the style and language employed in writing the minutes of meetings.

MCA (Revised) / BCA (Revised)
Term-End Examination

Chapter 14: Term-End Examination, December- 2017

MCS-015: COMMUNICATION SKILLS

Time: 2 hours
Maximum Marks: 50
Note: Answer all questions.

1. Read the following passage and answer the questions given below it: **10**

At this stage of civilization, when many nations are brought into close and vital contact for good and evil, it is essential, as never before, that their gross ignorance of one another should be diminished, that they should begin to understand a little of one another's historical experience and resulting mentality. It is the fault of the English to expect the people of other countries to react as they do, to political and international situations.
Our genuine goodwill and good intentions are often brought to nothing, because we expect other people to be like us. This would be corrected if we knew the history, not necessarily in detail but in broad outlines, of the social and political conditions which have given to each nation its present character. This knowledge about each other is also crucial for the fulfillment of the ultimate vision—one world, one family. We need to identify common elements and celebrate differences to really arrive at a stage when we treat each other not only as companions but also like family members. The spirit of family, faith, freedom, and sacrifice for the sake of sacrifice has to be the key.

(a) According to the author, what determines the 'mentality' of a nation? 2
(b) What is not right on the part of Englishmen? 2
(c) What are the values required to form a global family? 2
(d) What is the author's suggestion to all his fellow citizens? 2
(e) Pick out antonyms of the following words from the passage: 2
Fake, slavery

2. Do as directed: **5**
(a) The college is celebrating its Foundation Day next week.
(Rewrite in passive voice)

(b) We (must/should/ought) to respect traffic lights at all times.
(Select the appropriate modal)

(c) The girl was thirsty. The girl drank lime water.
(Combine these sentences)

(d) The match has been (called off/called up) by the umpires due to bad weather.
(Select the appropriate word)

(e) All men and women are rushing to the garment store. There (could/must) be a sale going on.
(Choose the suitable option)

3. Write a note in approximately 150 words on the format of minutes of a meeting. Emphasize the style and language used in writing it. 10

4. Prepare your Curriculum Vitae (CV) for the post of Sales Manager in response to the advertisement given below: 10

Position: Sales Manager, Infosys
Qualification: Bachelor's Degree in Business Administration with sound knowledge of the computer industry
Experience: Minimum 3 years in a reputed company
Job Profile: Managing Sales department at Bangalore office
Salary: As per industry standards

5. Prepare a report of the Industrial/Field visit that you went to. Also, mention the benefits that such visits lead to, specifically in terms of starting one's own enterprise. 15

MCA (Revised) / BCA (Revised)

Chapter 15: Term-End Examination, June- 2018

MCS-015: COMMUNICATION SKILLS

Time: 2 hours
Maximum Marks: 50
Note: Answer all questions. There are five questions.

1. Read the following passage and answer the questions given below it: **10**

If your desk is piled high with letters, faxes, memos, and print-outs, you might believe all this paperwork is a sign of how busy you are. But according to Declan Treacy, cluttered desks lead to lost information, distraction, missed opportunities, high stress, and not a little procrastination. He founded and runs the 'Clear Your Desk Day' Organization. His arguments for uncluttered desks are strong. We pile hundreds of pieces of paper on the desks with 45 minutes a day wasted on frustrating searches for lost paperwork on and around the desk. It is unfortunate that the cluttered desk is the accepted norm in most organizations, he says.

Paper has become the foundation on which our organizations are built. While a large proportion of this paperwork is important, most organizations, both public and private, are suffocating under mountains of unwanted paper. Each piece of paper on the desk distracts us up to five times a day. We habitually handle paperwork several times before deciding what to do with it. So what should they do if they have paper mountains on their desk? Dump it in the bin? Well yes, says Treacy. Or rather he suggests following four simple rules and dumping the stuff is number four. Rule number three is file it. Number two suggests passing it to someone else. Number one is the rule no one will like: act on it.

What you should not do is add to the pile of paper that's already there. Eighty percent of all paperwork is eventually discarded, but it causes an awful lot of trouble before that happens. Unfortunately, most executives believe the myth that an empty desk is the sign of an unproductive mind. How wrong can you be? Companies cannot afford to let people work from cluttered desks. Hours of valuable time are wasted in searching for vital pieces of paper and in being distracted by the constant stream of faxes, memos, and reports which land in our in-trays when we should be devoting time to more important work.

(a) Suggest a suitable title for the passage. 2
(b) According to the writer, what are the ill effects of having a cluttered desk? 2
(c) Find words in the passage which mean: 2
  (i) to take away attention
  (ii) throw away
(d) What are the arguments given in favor of an uncluttered desk? 2
(e) Enumerate the four rules for keeping one's desk clean. 2

2. Fill in the blanks choosing the most suitable phrasal verbs from those given below. (Make changes in verb form if necessary): 5

look into, look up, shut up, run across, fall behind, drop in

(a) They ___________ to him as their leader.
(b) Don't ___________ with your rent or you'll be evicted.
(c) Yesterday I ___________ my childhood friend.
(d) The judge promised to ___________ the matter.
(e) It is rude to ask people to ___________.

3. Write the text of a group discussion among three participants on the issue of whether political activities should be encouraged in educational institutions. 10

4. In response to an advertisement in 'The Times of India', write a job application along with your curriculum vitae for the job of an Accounts Officer in a leading multinational company. 10

5. Imagine you are working as a Personnel Manager in the Human Resource Department of IT Solutions. A system of flexible working hours has been proposed. Write a memo to the staff: 10

- Informing them about the proposed flexi-timings.
- Stating clearly that only Wednesdays and Thursdays would be the flexi-days in the initial stage.
- Telling them that there would be a core time between 1 pm and 3 pm when all members of the staff are supposed to be in the office.

MCA (Revised) / BCA (Revised)

Chapter 16: Term-End Examination, December- 2018

MCS-015: COMMUNICATION SKILLS

Time: 2 hours
Maximum Marks: 50
Note: There are five questions. Answer all questions.

1. Read the passage given below and answer the questions that follow: **10**

To meet and deal with life creatively, we need to be alert and thoughtful and think in a positive manner. We become what we imagine to be. No matter how insurmountable the task, with a positive attitude you can make a difference. Self-belief is quite the key ingredient in any success recipe. Mental richness can balance any situation. Positive thinking keeps tensions at bay and enables us to enjoy mental peace. A positive attitude will help in touching newer heights of professional success.

If we are intense in belief and in thought, we can stimulate immense personality forces into action. Inspiration and motivation must be replenished daily by a new intake of motivational thinking. Maintain an enthusiastic spirit at all times and under all conditions. The positive thinker alters his attitude of mind, constantly sends out positive thoughts, together with vital mental images of hope, optimism, and creativity leading to self-improvement, growth, and accomplishment. He does not react emotionally when in difficulty — being aware that only when the mind is cool, rational solutions are possible. A man who is self-reliant, positive, optimistic, and undertakes his work with the assurance of success magnetises his condition. He draws to himself the creative powers of the universe. Do the best, the very best you possibly can do. A chief duty of any of us is to endure what life brings. What cannot be avoided has to be endured.

(a) Give a suitable title to the passage. 2
(b) Mention two rewards of positive thinking. 2
(c) When a positive thinker is in difficulty, why does he refrain from reacting emotionally? 2
(d) Explain the statement 'Self-belief is quite the key ingredient in any success recipe. 2
(e) Pick out words from the passage which have the same meaning as the following: 2
    (i) that which cannot be overcome
    (ii) bear

2. Fill in the blanks in the following sentences by choosing the suitable phrasal verbs given below. There is one extra phrasal verb. (Make changes in the form of the verb where necessary): 5
Phrasal Verbs: play down, run down, put out, turn down, drop in, drop out

(a) Shiela tried to ___________ her son's faults.
(b) Aryan wanted to marry Sanya but she ___________ the proposal.

(c) Anil has ___________ of the cricket eleven.
(d) Some of my old friends ___________ for a cup of tea.
(e) One should always ___________ the lights before going out of the room.

3. Write down some of the points of a group discussion among three participants on the issue of the menace of stray dogs. 10

4. In response to an advertisement in 'The Hindustan Times', write an application for the job of Finance Controller in a leading multinational company. Also, attach your Curriculum Vitae (CV). 10

5. As a Marketing/Sales Executive of an automobile company, you have been asked to investigate the reason why there has been a drastic fall in the sale of cars. Write a report in about 250 words. 10

MCA (Revised) / BCA (Revised)

Chapter 17: Term-End Examination, June- 2019

MCS-015: COMMUNICATION SKILLS

Time: 2 hours
Maximum Marks: 50
Note: There are five questions. Answer all questions.

1. Read the passage given below and answer the questions that follow: 10

Working overseas is always a challenge for any professional and if you are an Indian, always strive to give your best as Indians have always been considered intelligent, hardworking, talented, and spiritual. Indians have always excelled in a competitive working environment and working overseas was something many Indians desired but few achieved till the information technology boom opened several white-collar job opportunities for them in global markets. However, while securing employment abroad may be an achievement, retaining it is quite a challenge as a professional requires constant demonstration of professionalism and exacting standards of competence. Then, there is this challenge of working in an alien environment coupled with numerous other variables like culture, people, work ethics, local regulations, etc., that one is expected to cope with to be successful on the job. Change, thus, becomes inevitable as one moves into a new work environment and the best way to tackle change is to be prepared for it and adapt to it rapidly.

(i) How have white-collar job opportunities been opened for Indians in the global markets? 2

(ii) Do you think retaining a job overseas is more difficult than getting one? Give reasons for your answer. 2

(iii) Find words in the passage which have the same meaning as the phrases/words given below: 2

Strange, certain to happen

(iv) Find words in the passage which are opposite in meaning to the words given below: 2

Material, lazy

(v) Give a suitable title to the passage. 2

2. Do as directed: 10

(i) She told that she wanted to become a teacher. *(Rewrite correctly)*

(ii) You (need not/must not) drive in the middle of the road. *(Fill in the blank with the correct option from the brackets)*

(iii) "Could you lend me your pen for a while, Ravi?" said Rajni. *(Rewrite in indirect speech)*

(iv) I am having five dogs in my house. *(Rewrite correctly)*

(v) He wrote two novels in one month. *(Rewrite in the passive voice)*

(vi) One of my brothers ______ a doctor. *(Fill in the blanks with a suitable word)*

(vii) He reached the airport. The flight had already left. *(Combine the two sentences)*

(viii) She is married, ______? *(Supply a suitable tag)*

(ix) He is so weak that he can't run fast. *(Rewrite using 'too')*

(x) All the clothes were washed and ironed by my mother. *(Rewrite in the active voice)*

3. You have taken a housing loan from a nationalized bank and you have been paying the interest at the rate prevailing at the time of borrowing. Post demonetization, write a letter to the Bank Manager to reduce the interest rate on your balance amount, in view of the announcement made in the Union Budget. 10

4. As the secretary of a students union, write the minutes of a meeting of the office bearers, held in connection with the annual function to be organized shortly. 10

5. As a sales executive of a publishing house, write a conversation with a client who wants to place a bulk order for textbooks for a chain of schools. (Ten turns in all) 10

MASTER OF COMPUTER APPLICATIONS (M.C.A.)

Chapter 18: Term-End Examination, December- 2019

MCS-015: COMMUNICATION SKILLS

Time: 2 Hours
Maximum Marks: 50
Note: Attempt all questions. All questions carry equal marks.

1. Read the passage given below and answer the questions that follow:
The daily explosion of crime, violence, and sex on the small screen reaches approximately one-third of the country's population. Fifty years ago, there was only one channel, Doordarshan. Now there are more than 50 channels. TV is no longer just a means for informing news, disseminating information, and building opinion. It is also for providing entertainment. The unfortunate development is that it has increasingly become the instrument for projecting crime, thrillers, horrors, vulgarity, and obscenity. Scenes of sex, crime, and violence capture the imagination of large sections of viewers, especially children, creating a disturbing impact on them.

Specialists have identified as many as 60 types of violence projected on TV, both audio and visual. These include slapping, threats, screaming, shooting, assaulting, abusing, pushing, stabbing, mental torture, eerie soundtracks, and threatening music. Most of the violence is explicit, graphic, and noticeably lengthy.

Children admire superheroes such as Shaktiman, who is capable of extraordinary physical feats; they tend to imbibe the exploits of such superheroes. Family drama serials also often depict conflicts involving violence. These include scenes of domestic violence, often involving children. There is an obvious tendency to glorify violence.

These circumstances need to be urgently considered by governmental authorities as well as social activists so that measures can be devised and adopted to mitigate the situation. These include persuading channels to adopt self-regulating measures, fixing times not earlier than 10 P.M. for serials and programs containing scenes of sex and violence, and avoiding repetitions of these shows at earlier times. Additionally, a written or verbal warning should be presented before such a program begins, and child-specific programs should be developed and telecast by all channels.

Questions:
(i) What do you understand by the term "Small Screen"? 1
(ii) What is the impact of TV programs on viewers? 2
(iii) Name one phrase used by the author for assaulting, stabbing, shooting, strangulating, abusing, pushing, etc. 1
(iv) Why do children like superheroes like Shaktiman? 2
(v) What is the harmful effect of feats of superheroes on children? 2
(vi) Why does the author suggest that certain serials/programs should not be telecast before 10 p.m.? 2

2. Do as directed: **10**

(i) A gang of thieves had raided the bank last night. (Rewrite correctly)

(ii) Children are innocent, ___? (Add a tag question)

(iii) Loud noise (effects, affects) our health adversely. (Fill in the blank choosing the appropriate word from the brackets)

(iv) This is the book ____. (Complete the sentence with a relative clause)

(v) One can't succeed in life unless one does not work hard. (Rewrite correctly)

(vi) "Why haven't you finished your homework till now, my son?" asked mother. (Rewrite in reported speech)

(vii) He said that his family was going to Bangalore the next day. (Rewrite in direct speech)

(viii) They demolished the old building in four hours. (Rewrite in the passive voice)

(ix) The paper is so long that I can't complete it in two hours. (Rewrite using 'too')

(x) He was head of the department ____ ten years. (Insert an appropriate preposition)

3. Write an online complaint to the relevant authority regarding the non-receipt of your AADHAAR card, which was processed six months back. 10

4. You are a company secretary of Escorts Ltd. Write the minutes of a recently held meeting of the sales team. 10

5. Write a dialogue between two friends who are planning a holiday. One of them is keen to join a hiking trip, and the other friend wishes to relax in Goa. Provide arguments from both sides, taking about 10 turns. 10

M.C.A. (REVISED) / B.C.A. (REVISED)

Chapter 19: Term-End Examination, June- 2020

MCS-015: COMMUNICATION SKILLS

Time: 2 Hours
Maximum Marks: 50
Note: Answer all questions.

1. Read the following passage and answer the questions given below it:
Passage

Brexit can lead to the development of a new form of the English language, according to an academic paper. Dr. Marko Modiano, of Gavle University in Sweden, said there were already signs that 'Euro-English' was developing its own distinct way of speaking. This may eventually be codified in a dictionary and taught in schools if English is retained as the lingua franca of the European Union after the U.K. leaves. The Europeans might also decide to adopt American spelling, Modiano said, which would add about 443 million to the total population using that system. Euro-English has already developed its own definitions for some words based on the 'Euro-speak' deployed in Brussels.
For example, 'eventual' is now used as a synonym for "possible or possibly," Modiano wrote in the journal 'World Englishes'. 'Subsidiarity' has come to mean "the principle that legal decrees should be enacted as close to people as possible," 'Brussels Brelaymone' means "bureaucracy," 'conditionality' means "conditions," and 'semester' means "six months."

Outside of Brussels, people are also developing their English sayings. "Phrases such as 'to hop over' (meaning 'to refrain from doing something'), 'to be blue-eyed' ('to be naive'), and 'to salt' ('to overcharge') are readily found among the usage of people in Nordic countries," Modiano said.

Grammar is also changing. For example, "I am coming from Spain" can be used to mean "I am from Spain" as part of the expansion of the use of -ing forms of verbs. And "we were five people at the party" means the same as "there were five people at the party." "Continental Europeans speaking English as a second language use this construction, 'we were' instead of 'there were'," Modiano said.

He said English was likely to remain as the EU lingua franca despite suggestions it should be abandoned with no member state having it as their official language. The EU will have only about five million native speakers of English after Brexit, representing about 1% of the population.

Questions:
(a) What is the nationality of Dr. Marko Modiano? 1
(b) How is the English language likely to be affected by Brexit (Britain's exit from the European Union)? 3

(c) Do you think Dr. Modiano's assumption is likely to come true? Give reasons for your answer. 2

(d) How will the sentence, "Mr. A belongs to France," be said in Euro-English? 2

(e) Locate words in the passage which have the following meanings: 2

(i) A shared language used by people whose main languages are different.

(ii) At the end of a period of time.

2. Do as directed: **5**

(a) The farmer is ploughing the field. (Rewrite in the passive voice)

(b) One (must to, ought to) respect one's parents. (Fill in the blank choosing the appropriate phrase from brackets)

(c) He went to bed with ___ bad cold. (Fill in the blank with an article if necessary)

(d) Anju (make) a dress for herself last week. She (make) all her own clothes. (Fill in the blanks with the correct form of verbs given in brackets)

(e) She is well-versed in classical music. Her voice is not sweet. (Combine the two simple sentences into one compound sentence)

3. In response to an advertisement in the Hindustan Times for the position of a Finance Controller, write an application for the same. Also, attach your curriculum vitae (C.V.). 15

4. What preparations should be made by a candidate before appearing for an interview? 10

5. What is the purpose of writing the minutes of a meeting? Discuss the abilities/skills required for writing minutes, giving examples where necessary. 10

M.C.A. (REVISED) / B.C.A. (REVISED)

Chapter 20: Term-End Examination, February- 2021

MCS-015: COMMUNICATION SKILLS

Time: 2 Hours
Maximum Marks: 50
Note: There are five questions. Answer all questions.

1. Read the passage given below and answer the questions that follow:
Passage:
It is probable that illness and infection caused by eating food contaminated with bacteria which produce diseases have existed since the beginning of time. Drinking water can be made safe by treating it with chlorine. Milk can be made safe by heating it and then packing it in sterilised containers. But it is either very difficult or simply not possible to treat most of the things we eat in either of these ways. All that can be done is either to prevent bacteria from entering food or to stop them from growing after they have entered.

For a long time, it was believed that some substances called ptomaines were the agents of food poisoning, but it was finally discovered that ptomaines, found in rotten food, can be swallowed without harmful effects following. In 1888, about 60 people, all of whom had eaten meat taken from the same animal, were taken ill, and one man died. Dr. Gaertner, a German bacteriologist, was able to isolate the food-poisoning bacteria which had caused the outbreak and put forward the theory that all food poisoning was due to the presence of such bacteria. This theory later became generally accepted, and between 1909 and 1923 many disease-producing bacteria were identified and given the name Salmonella, in honour of Dr. Salmon, who discovered the first member of the group.

In recent years, many more bacteria of this kind have been isolated and identified and probably many more will be discovered in the future. These bacteria may be present in small numbers in raw food; if they are not destroyed when the food is prepared or cooked, they multiply and make the food dangerous to eat.

Questions:
(i) Give an appropriate title to the passage and justify your answer. 2
(ii) How can drinking water and milk be made safe? 2
(iii) Why does the author think that the food we generally eat is difficult to save from getting contaminated? 2
(iv) How did Salmonella get its name? 1
(v) Use the following in sentences of your own: 3
Treat,Isolate, Identified

2. Do as directed: **5**
(i) The doctor examined the patient. (Rewrite in the passive voice)
(ii) I won't go out as it ________ (rain) and I ________ (not have) an umbrella. (Fill in the blanks with the correct form of verbs given in brackets)

(iii) "Mother has cooked tasty food today," said Aryan. (Rewrite in indirect speech)
(iv) There is ________ bag lying on ________ back seat of the car. (Fill in the blanks with appropriate articles)
(v) Nita was so tired that she could not do her homework. (Rewrite using "too")

3. In response to an advertisement in The Times of India, for the position of a Sales Manager in a reputed firm, write an application for the same. Also, attach your curriculum vitae (CV). 15

4. How is Group Discussion different from an Interview? Which mode would you prefer? Give reasons for your answer. 10

5. As a Company Secretary in an MNC, write the minutes of a meeting held to chalk out the plan for celebrating the Silver Jubilee of the company. 10

M.C.A. (REVISED) / B.C.A. (REVISED)

Chapter 21: Term-End Examination, June- 2021

MCS-015: COMMUNICATION SKILLS

Time: 2 Hours
Maximum Marks: 50
Note: Answer all questions.

1. Read the passage given below and answer the questions that follow:
Passage

BRIDGEHAMPTON. Friday. A disastrous fire broke out on the top floor of the Grand Hotel, Washington Road, in the small hours of the morning. The whole of the floor was gutted and damage estimated at £10,000 was done. Two of the guests staying at the hotel lost their lives.

Only one other casualty is reported. John Green (43) and his wife Emily Green (38) of London Rd., Acton, were trapped in their room and were evidently overcome by fumes before rescuers could reach them. A third guest, John Wills (63), of Leeds, was taken to hospital with multiple burns. His condition is reported as being serious. The alarm was given by the night porter, Robert Black, whose attention had been drawn to smoke issuing from one of the top floor windows by a group of young people returning late from a dance. Within five minutes the town Fire Brigade was on the spot.

The work of fighting the blaze and evacuating the by-now alarmed guests was seriously hampered by the non-operation of the lifts. It is believed that the fire was caused by a short circuit in the lift machinery and had extended to the whole floor before it was observed. The flames were brought under control in two hours. The manager, Mr. William Ramsey, interviewed by our reporter, expressed his deep regret at the loss of life and added, "It was lucky that the hotel was half empty at the time or we might have had more casualties."

Although it will be some months before the damage can be repaired, the hotel will remain open to guests as usual.

Questions:

(i) Why was it difficult to get the guests out of the hotel quickly? 2
(ii) How was the fire caused? 2
(iii) Who first noticed the fire? 2
(iv) Find words in the passage which are close in meaning to the following words/phrases:
Destroyed, Prevent from doing something 2
(v) Give a suitable title to the passage. 2

2. Do as directed: **10**

(i) You will never learn to be polite. (Change into an interrogative sentence)
(ii) In is more hotter today than yesterday. (Correct the sentence)
(iii) Your brother is a doctor, ... ? (Supply a suitable tag)

(iv) He completed his work much before the deadline. (Rewrite in the passive voice)
(v) The jewels have been stolen from the locker. (Rewrite in the active voice)
(vi) She went to England for .... studies. (Further, farther). (Fill in the blank with the appropriate word)
(vii) When I was young I use to walk very fastly. (Rewrite the sentence correctly)
(viii) We all .... (study) Sanskrit when we were in school. (Fill in the blank with the correct form of the verb)
(ix) She accused the servant .... stealing. (Insert an appropriate preposition in the blank)
(x) When ever I .... (go) to see him he was out. (Supply the correct form of the verb given in brackets)

3. Write a job application for the post of a Personnel Manager in a private firm. Attach a resume suitable for the job. Also, mention the source of your information regarding the vacancy. 10

4. As the Secretary of a well-known company, write the minutes of the meeting held to plan the celebration of Independence Day. 10

5. As Secretary of your Residents Welfare Association (RWA), write a letter to the municipal councillor to get the roads of the colony repaired. Also, draw his attention to the dog menace prevailing in the area. 10

M.C.A. (REVISED) / B.C.A. (REVISED)

Chapter 22: Term-End Examination, December- 2021

MCS-015: COMMUNICATION SKILLS

Time: 2 Hours
Maximum Marks: 50
Note: Attempt all questions.

1. Read the following passage and answer the questions given below it:
Passage
The average smartphone user checks her/his device 47 times a day. About 80% of smartphone users check their phones within one hour of their waking or going to sleep, 35% of which do so within five minutes in the given period. Around 70% of Internet use by people in the workplace has nothing to do with their jobs. These statistics clearly prove our increasing addiction to the Internet and our smartphones as well as our need for remedial action. It is easy to pin the blame on technology; 'it has spoiled us'. But the fact is technology is neutral; it does not tell us how to wisely or unwisely use or misuse it. Our focus should be on using technology to improve our well-being. For instance, one can use 'Nightshift', an app for improving sleep, or one can use smart tools such as 'Do Not Disturb' feature which enables blocking of calls and notifications for a set period in a day. Other than using technology, one can also exercise self-control and self-discipline to regulate the usage time of their cellphones.

Initially, cellphones helped to add more value and ease to our real practical worldly life. Very soon, however, things changed drastically. Social media became a pair of rose-tinted glasses. It was used to show off instead of reflecting reality. You know things are not OK with you but you are deceptively led to believe that everyone else is having a great time and you are the only unfortunate one facing misfortunes.

Under the circumstances, only you can decide when to use or not to use the phone. Let it not dominate and regulate your life. Even when you get bored don't surrender. Think of an alternative. You can end up being creative. Life has endless possibilities. There is no such thing as one remedy suits all. Each individual is unique and so should be her/his remedial action, least of which, is dependence on the cell phone.

Questions:
(i) How often do most of the people use the cell phone? 2
(ii) Does the writer appreciate the frequent use of cell phones? Give reasons for your answer. 2
(iii) In the context of the passage, explain the sentence, "Very soon things changed drastically." 2
(iv) What does the pronoun 'it' refer to in the sentence 'Let it not dominate and regulate your life'? 2
(v) Complete the sentence: To overcome boredom, one of the alternatives suggested by the writer to the use of cell phone is 2

2. Do as directed: **10**

(i) The announced the arrival of the train over the loudspeaker. (Rewrite in the passive voice)
(ii) He was allowed ten minutes to get ready. (Rewrite in the active voice)
(iii) She has completed her graduation, ... ? (Supply a suitable question tag)
(iv) Do you think that is a good firm to invest .... ? (Insert an appropriate preposition)
(v) This is the best of the two books. (Rewrite the sentence correctly)
(vi) There was no one to listen to her appeal. (Change into an interrogative sentence)
(vii) My brother .... (use to, used to) participate in many games when he was young. (Fill in the blanks choosing the correct word from the brackets)
(viii) If I .... (was, were) the Finance Minister I would abolish all taxes. (Fill in the blanks choosing the correct word from the brackets)
(ix) He had already .... (speak) for an hour and he .... (go) on for another whole one. (Fill in the blanks with the correct tense of the verbs given in brackets)

3. In response to an advertisement for the post of a Marketing Manager in a well-known company, write a letter of application for the same. Also, write a suitable curriculum vitae. 10

4. As the Secretary of the English Study Circle, write an email to all the members informing them about the date, time, and venue of the annual general body meeting. 10

5. You want to seek an appointment with the Personnel Manager of a business house. Develop a telephone conversation with his/her secretary. 10

M.C.A. (REVISED) / B.C.A. (REVISED)

Chapter 23: Term-End Examination, June- 2022

MCS-015: COMMUNICATION SKILLS

Time: 2 Hours
Maximum Marks: 50
Note: There are five questions. Answer all questions.

1. Read the following passage and answer the questions given below it:
Passage
Beggars are a common sight in India. They are found at all crowded places. Many of them are hideously disfigured to arouse pity in people. Some of them are very persistent and annoying. They are known also to hurl curses and abuses at those who do not give them anything. They may seem to have no self-respect as they whine and cajole others into paying them.

Why do people beg? After all, it is degrading for anyone to have to beg. Poverty and widespread unemployment compel people to pass days and days without food. Hunger drives them to beg for their food. Later it becomes a habit.

Besides poverty, laziness is another reason. Begging, to some people, appears to be easier than doing honest work. Many beggars are rich. Kidnapping children makes them rich and idle. Beggary is a social evil. It degrades human beings to the level of whining, whimpering parasites, robbing them of all vestiges of self-respect.

In order to remove this blot from our society, the government may help a lot. The first step is to provide food, shelter, and employment to the beggars. Giving and asking for alms should be banned by law. The beggars should be assured of the basic necessities of life.

Answer the following questions:
(a) Give an appropriate title to the passage. 2
(b) Why do some beggars seem to be annoying instead of being objects of pity? 2
(c) What are the major reasons for begging? 2
(d) What are the negative impacts of begging? 2
(e) What can the government do to stop begging? 2

2. Rewrite as directed: **5**
(a) A book of short stories is lying on the table. This was written by the famous writer Anton Chekhov. (Combine the above sentences into one sentence using 'which')
(b) I reached the Mall for shopping. I did not realise that it ___________ (close). (Write the correct form of the verb)
(c) My next novel will be published in 2022 by a new publisher. (Change the voice)
(d) Rohan ran home after college. He wanted to share the news about his scholarship with his parents. (Join the sentences using a conjunction)
(e) I wants to go to my friend house. (Correct the sentence, if necessary)

3. Write an application in response to an advertisement in the Times of India for the position of Content Writer. Also, attach your Curriculum Vitae (CV). 15

4. What important steps should be taken in the course of preparing for an interview? 10

5. What do you understand by the term 'minutes'? Discuss giving appropriate examples. 10

M.C.A. (REVISED) / B.C.A. (REVISED)

Chapter 24: Term-End Examination, December- 2022

MCS-015: COMMUNICATION SKILLS

Time: 2 Hours
Maximum Marks: 50
Note: There are five questions. Answer all questions.

1. Read the following passage and answer the questions given below it:
Passage
The singlemost important guideline to keep in mind when tackling learning problems is this: do not let your learning difficulties get in the way of being a successful human being. The problem with the term 'learning disabled' is that the learner might overidentify with it and begin to see himself/herself as a handicapped individual. This can have a devastating effect upon one's self-worth. See yourself as an intact and whole human being before anything else. Then regard your learning difficulties simply as something that makes you an even richer and more unique human being.

Many successful individuals with learning problems have discovered that they can bypass their difficulties and find alternative ways of getting the job done. The famed inventor and industrialist Henry Ford had difficulty reading and remembering facts. He built a multi-million dollar empire by overcoming these difficulties in a different way. He surrounded himself with people who could answer any question he desired to ask, concerning the business to which he was devoting most of his effort. As he himself said, "Why should I clutter up my mind with general knowledge for the purpose of being able to answer questions, when I have men around me who can supply any knowledge I require?"

Answer the following questions:
(a) Give a suitable title to the passage. 2
(b) What is the best remedy to tackle learning problems? 2
(c) What is the most worrying aspect of the term 'learning disabled'? 2
(d) How can 'learning problems' be overcome successfully? 2
(e) Find synonyms of the word 'harmful' from the passage. 2

2. Rewrite as directed: 5
(a) The gardener is watering the plants. (Rewrite in the passive voice)
(b) One _______ (must, ought to) respect traffic rules. (Choose the appropriate word/phrase from the options given in the brackets)
(c) He woke up in the morning with _______ bad throat. (Fill in the blank with an article, if necessary)
(d) She has got training in classical music. Her voice is also suitable for that. (Combine the two sentences into one compound sentence)
(e) Roshni _______ (make) a Chinese dish for the party. She ________ (make) something special every time her friends come to see her. (Fill in the correct form of verbs given in the brackets)

3. Write an application in response to an advertisement in the newspaper, The Tribune, for the position of Bank Manager. Also, attach your Curriculum Vitae (CV). 15

4. Discuss the role and qualities of a good negotiator. 10

5. A private limited company is keen to buy 100 computers and 50 printers. Write a conversation between the Sales Head of WIPRO and the Manager of the private limited company regarding the availability of computers and printers, software specifications, price and discount, after-sale services, etc. 10

M.C.A. (REVISED) / B.C.A. (REVISED)

Chapter 25: Term-End Examination, June- 2023

MCS-015: COMMUNICATION SKILLS

Time: 2 Hours
Maximum Marks: 50
Note: Answer all questions.

1. Read the passage given below and answer the questions that follow:
Today's youth wants name, fame, and affluence without putting in the required efforts. They run after jobs and aspire to high salaries. They are not very keen to start small businesses of their own. They may argue that it requires money. But banks are ready to fund their projects. The other argument can be that it requires practical knowledge. But one can work part-time or as an intern in some firm to gain practical knowledge. The government also provides training to upcoming entrepreneurs willing to start their own business. One's own business can be a grocery shop, a coaching center, a computer institute, or so on. The success of the venture very much depends on the entrepreneur's ability, hard work, dedication, and grit. So, one should not wait for an ideal job but think of starting one's own business. One has to climb the steps slowly and steadily to reach the apex. It may help them to lead a stable and normal life and acquire a good career.

Questions:

(a) According to the author, what troubles the understanding of today's youth? 2
(b) What are the two important factors for running one's own business? 2
(c) What determines the success of an entrepreneur? 2
(d) What is the piece of advice given by the author to today's youth? 2
(e) Suggest a suitable title for the passage. 2

2. Do as directed: 5
(a) I will clean the entire house every Saturday. (Rewrite in passive voice)
(b) I .... run faster when I was younger. (Use the appropriate modal)
(c) The student was hard-working. The student won the first prize in the final examinations. (Combine the two sentences)
(d) All the tickets of the football match have been .... (sold away, sold out)
(e) When she fell ill, her son .... her. (looked after, looked before)

3. Write a note in approximately 150 words on the format of taking down the minutes of a meeting. Underline the do's and don'ts in making the minutes most communicative. 10

4. You have seen the advertisement for the position of Systems Analyst with a multinational company in a national newspaper. Prepare a suitable CV/Resume to apply for the position. 10

5. You have been asked by the Principal/In-charge to write a report based on the survey of the views of staff and students regarding the physical and technological upgradation of the institution. Prepare the report. 15

9 789369 721498

Printed at Repro India Ltd.